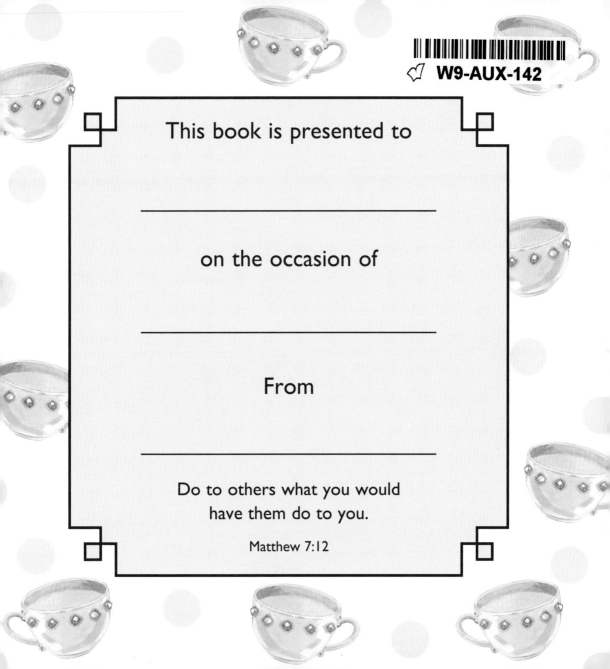

This book is presented to

_____

on the occasion of

_____

From

_____

Do to others what you would
have them do to you.

Matthew 7:12

Good Manners for a Little Princess

By Kelly Chapman
Illustrated by Tammie Lyon

HARVEST HOUSE PUBLISHERS

EUGENE, OREGON

To my beautiful queen mum—
The way you persevere as you battle
the pink ribbon disease truly inspires me.
You're a living example of Philippians
4:13, "I can do all this through him who
gives me strength."
I love you, Mom.

Good Manners for a Little Princess

Text Copyright © 2011 by Kelly Chapman
Artwork Copyright © 2011 by Tammie Lyon

Published by Harvest House Publishers
Eugene, Oregon 97402
www.harvesthousepublishers.com

ISBN 978-0-7369-3723-8

Design and production by Mary pat Design, Westport, Connecticut

Made with nontoxic inks and coatings (CPSIA compliant).

Printed in China

11 12 13 14 15 16 17 18 / **LP** / 10 9 8 7 6 5 4 3 2 1

What is Princess Prep School?
For more information, please visit
www.royalpurpose.com

Chapter One—Manners Matter

Once upon a *real* time, there lived a girl named Caroline. She loved everything princess. She even dreamed of one day teaching others how to be true, forever princesses. But there was one problem. Caroline and her friends thought learning about sparkling crowns and princess gowns was more important than learning about manners. In fact, they didn't think manners mattered much at all. What do you think?

Let's find out what is true about manners.

A Princess Teatime

"Gather around! I have a special surprise for you today," announced Miss Lily, a Princess Prep School teacher. "Since you have worked so hard on your service project this week, we're going to have a tea party!"

"I knew all *my* hard work would pay off," bragged Prissy Crissy, who thought she knew everything about everything.

"You mean all *our* hard work," corrected Missy, Caroline's best friend.

"Missy's right! It was a group effort," Caroline added.

"Miss Lily, will there be any scrumptious, deliyumcious tea cakes?" asked Kendall, Caroline's younger sister.

"It wouldn't be a tea party without them," laughed Miss Lily. "Why don't we start by…"

Before Miss Lily could finish her sentence the girls took off. They ran to the table. Missy reached it first and was about to sit down when someone grabbed her chair.

"I want to sit here!" demanded Prissy Crissy.

"Well, I got here first!" replied Missy as she quickly grabbed her chair back and sat down.

"Fine!" Prissy Crissy huffed. She sat down in the next chair. "I get to have the first tiara tea cake though!" She reached across Missy's plate for the platter with the tea cakes.

"Too late!" Kendall shouted, her mouth already full of cake.

"How do you like my tiara?" Kimmy asked as she balanced a tiara tea cake on her head.

"Pink princess tea is my favorite!" Caroline exclaimed as she slurped her last sip.

"And it's fun to drink too," Kendall said as she enthusiastically blew air through the straw to make the pink princess tea bubble.

Missy nodded her head as she took a huge bite of her tea cake. Because she was chewing with her mouth open, a little bit fell out and landed on the table. "Oops!" she said.

"These tea cakes really are so...so...achoo!" Missy sneezed all over her food. "They're so delicious," she continued. "You should try one," she said as she took another humongous bite.

"Miss Lily, are you going to join us for tea?" Caroline asked. She sat on her knees in her chair so she'd be taller.

"I'm afraid not," said Miss Lily. "I lost my appetite watching all of you eat. There's an important list I need to make right now."

"Is it a list of what we're supposed to do for our service project?" Kimmy asked.

"Actually, it's a list of what you're not supposed to do," answered Miss Lily. "This list will help all of you in your royal responsibilities, including your service project."

Miss Lily sat down at the table and wrote for a few minutes. When she was done, she looked up and said, "Okay, princesses, watching you at the tea party reminded me of something we need to talk about. I've made an important list that I've titled 'Royally Wrong Manners.' I've written 12 things that should *not* be done when sitting down to eat. And all 12 of these bad manners were committed at today's tea party. Before I share the list, can anyone guess what the 12 bad manners are?"

The girls looked at each other, and then they all shook their heads.

Miss Lily nodded. "I was afraid you wouldn't know them. I'll read them to you."

Royally Wrong Manners

1. Demanding your own seat.
2. Not washing your hands before eating.
3. Not praying before eating.
4. Reaching across the table.
5. Talking with your mouth full of food.
6. Playing with your food.
7. Slurping your drink.
8. Blowing bubbles in your drink.
9. Chewing your food with your mouth open.
10. Not covering your mouth when you sneeze.
11. Taking bites of food that are too big.
12. Sitting on your knees in your chair.

"I saw these being done, so I think it's important we spend some time learning about manners," said Miss Lily.

"Manners? Only boys need to learn about good manners!" declared Prissy Crissy.

"Yeah. Girls are born with them," added Kendall as she wiped her mouth on her sleeve.

"Isn't it more important to learn about our royal responsibilities?" Kimmy asked.

"Besides, manners don't *really* matter," Caroline said, still sitting on her knees in her chair. She reached for her teacup. "Oh!" she cried as she fell out of the chair and landed with a thud on the floor.

Miss Lily got up and rushed over to Caroline. "Caroline, are you all right?" she asked.

"She looks like a sleeping princess," Kendall said.

Lying unconscious on the floor, Caroline began dreaming a dreamy kind of dream where the skies are bluer, the pinks are pinker, and the castles are heavenly. She dreamed that she and her sister and friends were invited to attend Princess Prep School at the Castle of Calvary. Their teacher was Miss Lily, who was now a real princess, living in a real castle, once upon a real time.

"Hear ye! Hear ye! I have an important message to relay. Tomorrow's princess lesson will be taught in a mannerly way," declared Constant, the king's royal helper. "The table will be set for a special kind of tea that is full of surprises, as you will soon see."

"Constant's right! Tomorrow we're going to have a mannerly kind of tea party!" confirmed Princess Lily. "Be sure to wear your fanciest tutu because I have a surprise for all of you."

Kendall was overjoyed. That night she was too excited to sleep. But she finally drifted off, and before she knew it, morning arrived.

"Rise and shine!" shouted Caroline as she jumped onto Kendall's bed. "What do you think of the fancy tutu I picked out to wear?"

"Hey, that's the one I wanted to wear!" complained Kendall. "It's my favorite, and I want to look the fanciest!" she growled.

"Fine, I'll let you because you're my little sister, but you don't have to be so cranky about it," Caroline responded. She handed Kendall the tutu.

"Who's cranky?" asked Kimmy as she walked into the room.

"I was just teasing Kendall," answered Caroline. "It seems like *someone* woke up on the wrong side of the bed."

Caroline ran back into her room and put on a different tutu. Then she went back into Kendall's room. "I'm ready," she announced.

"Maybe the tea party will cheer her up," suggested Missy. "Last one there is a rotten princess!"

All three girls took off, running through the bedroom doorway.

"And stop calling me names!" yelled Kendall as she slammed her bedroom door shut, accidentally catching her tutu in it.

Rrrrrriiiiiipppp!

"Wahhhh!" wailed Kendall. "Look at what you made me do!" She jerked open the door and went back into her room to put on a different outfit. Then she headed for the tearoom. The closer she got to the banquet hall, the crankier she became.

"It's all Caroline's fault!" Kendall declared as soon as she entered the tearoom. "She made me rip my favorite tutu!"

"All I did was call her cranky for waking up on the wrong side of the bed," defended Caroline.

"I can't help it if I was too excited to sleep last night. Caroline didn't have to tease me!" replied Kendall as she stomped her foot.

"Girls, this is no way for true, forever princesses to behave," Princess Lily said, interrupting the feud. "As true, forever princesses, we have the royal responsibility of using good manners because we represent the King of kings. Manners show people what's inside our hearts. If we have bad manners, we're telling people we don't respect them or ourselves. Did you know the Bible has a lot to say about manners? And I'm afraid all of you have broken one of the main Bible principles. It's called the 'Golden Rule,' which is a truth we get from the Bible. Matthew 7:12 says, 'So in everything, do to others what you would have them do to you.' Treating others the way we want to be treated is an important rule to live by. That's why it's called the Golden Rule."

"How can we keep from breaking this rule?" asked Caroline.

"By loving God and loving others," answered Princess Lily. "In fact, Jesus said that loving God and loving people are the most important things we are to do."

"That's too hard!" exclaimed Kendall. "Especially when someone calls you cranky." She glared at Caroline.

"You're right. It is hard," agreed Princess Lily. "In fact, it's impossible without God's help. That's why we need to pray and ask Him to help us love others. When we do, we become a 'Golden Rule Keeper' instead of a 'Golden Rule Breaker.' The choice is up to each of us. Which one do you want to be? Let's make a list and show what the differences are," Princess Lily said. She went to the chalkboard and wrote for a few minutes. "Okay, girls. Let's read this together."

Golden Rule Keeper

Loves God...

Loves others..

Treats others the way she
wants to be treated...

Shakes hands, makes eye contact..................

Respects and shares with everyone...........

Waits her turn to talk.......................................

Takes turns...

Shares..

Speaks truthfully..

Golden Rule Breaker

Loves herself and brags

Thinks of herself first

Teases, pushes, and shoves

Keeps hands in pockets, slouches

Whispers to one person in a group

Acts rudely and interrupts

Cuts in line

Acts selfishly

Lies

The girls looked over the list. They realized they
hadn't been acting in a loving way toward each other.
They quickly apologized and forgave each other for
breaking the Golden Rule.

"Princess Lily, we've all decided we want to be Golden Rule Keepers!" Caroline announced.

"Now that's spoken like true, forever princesses!" Princess Lily said as she smiled. "I think we're ready to start our tea party. What do you say?"

"Zzzzzz."

Kendall's head was on the table, and her eyes were closed.

"Maybe it's best we let the sleeping beauty rest," Princess Lily said. "When she wakes up, I'll reveal a surprise."

Kendall woke up when she heard the word "surprise." She didn't want to miss a thing.

As the girls entered the banquet hall, they were stunned. All the plates and teacups and silverware were scattered everywhere on the table and turned upside down.

"Surprise!" exclaimed Princess Lily.

"Constant must have been in a big hurry," Caroline said. "What a mess."

"Actually, he set the table this way on purpose," Princess Lily stated. "We wanted to surprise you with a Pretty Please Princess Tea Party!' You'll soon discover that this isn't just any kind of tea party. It's an 'upside down, spin it around as you learn how to wear your crown' kind of tea party.

"We'll begin with table place setting manners. Let's see if you know how to arrange your place setting—your glass, plate, spoon, fork, knife, and napkin—properly. You have two minutes starting...now!" Princess Lily said looking at her watch.

"This is going to be easy smeasy!" bragged Prissy Crissy. "I'm an expert at being a proper princess, you know."

"Time's up!" announced Princess Lily.

"I'm afraid none of these settings are correct," Princess Lily said. "Let's ring for Constant and have him show us the right way to set a table. Watch and learn as he shows us where each piece goes."

As he worked, Constant sang,

> Setting the table can be easy as one, two, three,
> Just follow these steps, and you will agree.
> First you take your plate and place it on the table,
> Then top it with your napkin, and fold it, if you're able.
> Next place your dinner fork to the left side of your plate,
> With your salad fork by its side as if it were its mate.
> Then gently place your knife by your plate on the right
> To its side goes your teaspoon that's smaller in height.
> Your glass crowns your plate on the upper-right side,
> Now you can set the table with confidence and pride.

"Okay, princesses. Now it's your turn," Princess Lily said.

The girls got to work and were soon done.

"That wasn't so hard—thanks to you, Constant," said Caroline.

"How very kind, Caroline," replied Constant. "Thank you." He walked around the table and poured everyone pink princess tea.

"Now that you know how to set the table, it's time to test your teatime etiquette. Here is the 'Pretty Please Princess Tea Pop Quiz.'" Princess Lily passed out the quiz. "This little test is to see how much you know about table manners. There are five multiple-choice questions. Circle the answers you think are correct."

(Dear Reader, you can take this test along with Caroline and Kendall and the other girls if you like. You can find the test at the very back of this book.)

Princess Lily, why do we have to know so many table manners?" asked Kendall as she reached across the table for a tea cake, knocking over a full cup of pink princess tea and spilling it all over Prissy Crissy's tutu and shoes.

"Oh! Now I know why we need to practice good table manners,"
Kendall exclaimed.

Chapter Four—Princess Pleasantries

"This might be the perfect time to talk about another manner that really matters when it comes to getting along with others," said Princess Lily. "We call it 'Princess Pleasantries.'"

"Well, I'm not feeling very pleasant right now!" complained Prissy Crissy. "My tutu and my shoes are a sticky mess thanks to Kendall!"

"Kendall, when we accidentally do something to someone or hurt them with our words or actions, we say 'I'm sorry' and ask the person to forgive us," Princess Lily said gently.

"Okay. I'm sorry, Prissy Crissy. But you don't have to throw a hissy fit," Kendall said. "Your tutu and shoes will dry. So do you forgive me?"

"Kendall, that's not the kind of apology I'm talking about," Princess Lily explained quickly before Prissy Crissy could respond. "A true apology comes from a thoughtful heart that is truly sorry. Why don't you try again?"

"Oh. Okay. I'm sorry, Prissy Crissy, for accidentally spilling my tea on your tutu," apologized Kendall. "I'd like to help you clean it off. Will you forgive me?"

"Yes, I forgive you because I know you didn't mean to do it," said Prissy Crissy.

"That was much better," encouraged Princess Lily. "Saying 'I'm sorry' and forgiving each other are a part of having good princess manners. Other good words to use are 'please' and 'thank you.' They show that we respect others. Now let's see how many Princess Pleasantries words you can name in the next ten seconds. Ready, set, go!"

"Hello and good-bye!" yelled Caroline.

"Yes, sir and no, sir!" said Missy.

"Yes, ma'am and no, ma'am!" echoed Kimmy.

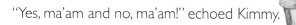

"No thank you, but it sure looks delicious!" exclaimed Kendall.

"Pretty please!" shouted Prissy Crissy.

"Excuse me!" Missy yelled.

"Nice to meet you," Caroline added.

"Time's up!" said Princess Lily. "Wow, ten words in ten seconds. That's really great. Girls, you're ready for the next step. I think you'll be pleasantly surprised! Finish up your tea and tea cakes. Crissy, why don't you run to the restroom and clean up. Kendall, did you want to help her?"

"Yes, I'll help!"

The two girls left together. Five minutes later they returned, smiling and laughing.

"Okay, now that we're all here, please follow me to the palace ballroom," Princess Lily announced.

Chapter Five—The Tutu Trot Review

"Wow! This ballroom was made for twirling!" exclaimed Kendall.

"You're absolutely right, Kendall," said Princess Lily. "This room was made for twirling, singing, and dancing. In fact, this is the biggest room in the Castle of Calvary. This is where we have special gatherings to praise Jesus."

"I thought we only praised Jesus in church," Kendall said.

"We do praise Jesus in church, Kendall. But we don't have to stop there. In fact, we're supposed to praise Jesus in everything we do and wherever we go. Did you know that our actions, words, and even manners bring praise to Him too?"

"Uh oh. I'd better learn good manners then," Kendall decided. "But what if I can't remember them all? What if I make a mistake?"

"That is the very reason why I brought you to the palace ballroom," Princess Lily announced. "I have a dance that will help you remember good manners. It's called 'The Tutu Trot.' Follow along!"

As Princess Lily danced, she sang a song with the instructions for the steps.

The Tutu Trot
Let's trot like a horse to review our manners course.
Now twirl to the right to remember to be polite.
Next spin around again to always be a friend.
Then pretend to swim in a pool to keep the "Golden Rule."
Now trot around some more as we circle about the floor.
Next take a little spin to start the review again.
Now stop and freeze and remember to cover when you sneeze.
Then fly like a dove to remember to always love.
Wave your hands in the air before you eat to say a prayer.
Now trot around again and curtsey to your friend.

"Can we do the dance again?" asked Prissy Crissy. "Kendall kept bumping into me."

The girls took their positions as Princess Lily started the Tutu Trot again. Everything was going fine until Kendall began to spin out of control. She kept twirling and twirling until she twirled right into Caroline, who twirled right into a chair.

"Well, I guess this is one way tutu take a break," joked Caroline as she sat on her knees in the chair. As Caroline laughed she accidently fell out of the chair. *Wham!* She fell on the floor and lay still.

Caroline heard someone calling her name. She slowly opened her eyes and looked up. Miss Lilly was looking down at her.

"Caroline, are you okay?" she asked. The girls were gathered around them both.

"What happened?" Caroline asked as she sat up.

"You fell out of your chair," Miss Lily said.

"I guess manners *really* do matter." Caroline rubbed her head. "Who knew that sitting on your knees in a chair could be so dangerous? From now on I'm going to sit straight in my chair with my feet on the floor!"

"That's a good idea! Girls, Caroline's right. Manners do matter. That's why we're going to spend some time learning about manners with a 'Pretty Please Princess Tea,'" Miss Lily announced.

"Will we get to dance the Tutu Trot?" asked Caroline.

"I've never heard of the Tutu Trot," Miss Lily said, looking at Caroline. "Will you teach it to us?"

"Me? Teach the Tutu Trot in a princess class? Wow! Dreams really do come true!" Caroline exclaimed.

Pretty Please Princess Tea Pop Quiz

This little test is to see how much you know about table manners.
There are five multiple-choice questions. Circle the answers you think are correct.

While sitting at the tea party table...

1. When is it okay to start eating?

a. As soon as you sit down.

b. After you've washed your hands, everyone's seated, and you've prayed.

c. When you're hungry.

d. As soon as you get your favorite food.

2. What do you do with your napkin?

a. Make funny-shaped animals with it.

b. Napkin? That's what sleeves are for!

c. Do magic tricks with it to entertain everyone.

d. Place it in your lap.

3. When is it okay to play with your food?

a. Never.

b. When you're finished eating.

c. When you're eating spaghetti.

d. When you don't like the food.

4. When is it okay to talk with food in your mouth?

a. When you have something to say.

b. When you want to show someone what color your food is.

c. Never.

d. When you want more food.

5. What do you do when you are finished eating?

a. Demand dessert.

b. Lick your plate to get every delicious drop of food.

c. Jump up from the table and go play.

d. Ask to be excused.

"Let's see how you did. Let's go over the correct answers," Princess Lily said.

- For question 1, the correct answer is *b: After you've washed your hands, everyone's seated, and you've prayed.*
- The correct answer for question 2 is *d: Place it in your lap.*
- The correct answer for question 3 is *a: Never.*
- The correct answer for question 4 is *c: Never.*
- The correct answer for question 5 is *d: Ask to be excused.*